stepping stones II

MARK GREGSTON

"Dedicated to Bill & Susanne Walsh,
Roger & Lori Kemp and
James and Kathy MacDonald...
true friendship is a gift from the Lord.

Stepping Stones II: Wisdom and Encouragement for your Parenting Journey
Copyright 2012 by Mark Gregston
Published by The Heartlight Ministries Foundation
P.O. 480
Hallsville, Texas 75650

Hope…when parenting feels hopeless.	6
Faith…in what you know to be true.	20
Trust…what you've taught & His presence in the life of your child.	36
Commitment…to do what is right.	54
Patience…in doing what you know is right	74
Loving When It's Hard…and you're ready to give up.	94
Restoration of relationships you hold dear.	110

contents

ced.

If you have children living at home, I challenge you to read a passage in the Bible… First Thessalonians, chapter 5.

Read these verses… and imagine them as directives to you as a mom or dad. Be joyful always, pray continually, give thanks in all circumstances, for this is God's will for you in Christ Jesus. Sounds like a tall order, doesn't it? Especially when there's tension at home that almost always accompanies adolescents.

But my hope for you is that you'll see this period in your life as the very thing that transforms you. When you come to the end of yourself— as you always will in parenting— fall on the grace of God… and find that He's changing you for the better!

And that's good cause for "giving thanks in all circumstances"!

hope

What makes a good parent?

I work with a lot of kids at our residential counseling center in Texas, called Heartlight. And after years of meeting with hurting parents and teens, I've seen over and over again that moms and dads are really trying to be good parents. And they are!

But in their zeal to care for their kids and protect them from a harmful world… they end up suffocating them, instead. So, let me, first, affirm that your love and commitment are wonderful. Keep it up.

But, second, let the reigns out a little bit for your child. The values you've built into them so far will help them survive in the world. Just keep loving them… and avoid the temptation to smother.

When you're tempted to control …let 'em go!

stepping stones II

I run across lots of parents who want to "have it all together." In fact, they want the world to know that they have it all together! You and I know, however, that no one's perfect.

Perfection can seem attainable in the idyllic early- childhood years, when kids are still adorable. But as children grow, families must begin that slow transformation into a home that allows… and encourages… imperfection.

It may come out in the way we present ourselves to our kids… making sure they know we make mistakes and ask for forgiveness when we do. Then, try and foster an atmosphere of acceptance in your home… for all the imperfections that come with being human.

h o p e

One day your son or daughter will walk out the door… will find a job or go to college… and the true test of your parenting skills begins!

 At that point, when your teen strikes out on their own, it won't matter if his room is clean, or what music she listened to. It won't matter if he watched too much TV or if she didn't study as much as she should.

What will matter is whether your child is still dependent on you to make it in life. Has he developed skills to face the demands of adulthood? Has your relationship equipped her to be independent?

Mom… Dad… start now. Start preparing your child for the day they'll walk out that door and out from under your care. Foster independence now… so they'll stand strong when they're on their own!

stepping stones II

Don't give up hope parents! Just because you'll never be able to compete with what the world has to offer your kids, you have the opportunity to give your kids what they want and cannot receive from anyone or anything else in their life. From you they will receive value that no one else can give, accentuated by the time that you give them. They can have experiences that they'll laugh and cry about the rest of their lives. And in the midst of it all, they'll gain wisdom in a way that can only be offered by you.

It's all because of the relationship that you have with them. That's why your relationship with them is so important.

hope

Mom …Dad …let me guess… if you have teens under your roof, I'll venture to say that conflict is a regular part of your home. Right?

Whether it comes in the form of intense debate … or even prolonged silence… there's no getting around the natural tension in any family. Its just part of life.

So every parent needs to decide ahead of time …how will you respond when things get messy? A good intentional plan will help you keep your cool …and also help your kids learn to deal with inevitable conflicts that await them in the real world.

Make no mistake. You don't do your kids any favors by teaching them to run from disagreements. When you disengage from conflict… the greatest agent of change has just left the building!

stepping stones II

If you're raising a teenager, then here's the first thing you can take to the bank: Teenagers will act like teenagers during their teenage years!

Yep, your kids will make mistakes. They'll lie. They'll mistreat people. They'll stumble. But just because they mess up from time to time doesn't mean we bail them out of their consequences.

The second thing you can count on is this: what you've taught your kids is paramount. The seeds you've sown in their lives will one day come to fruition!

And third: mom and dad… trust God's involvement in your kid's life! He wants good things for your teen. And He'll never abandon you or your kids.

Take those three things to the bank and cash them in! Some day your teen will thank you.

hope

What if my kid's behavior is driving me nuts? That was a question posed to me some time ago by a frantic parent.

This particular mom was dealing with a teen who was extremely selfish, didn't respect authority, expressed anger, had Attention Deficit Disorder and constantly blamed others for his behavior. Sounds like a handful, doesn't he?

Well, I would tell any parent with a struggling teen the same thing I told this particular mom. Resist the tendency to lump everything together into one huge and overwhelming mess. It compounds his belief that things will never get better!

Instead, stick to what you believe. Stand firm in your rules and consequences. Keep your cool. And know that you will get to the other side of this. There is hope!

In order for parents to have a healthy relationship with their teen… it's necessary to create a safe harbor where healthy relationships can develop. So… does your child sense your unconditional love?

Relationships thrive in an atmosphere of unqualified acceptance. That means… even when your child blows it big time, or doesn't respond the way you'd like …you don't threaten to abandon him. He knows, without question, that your love is forever.

Every teen has a secret longing to belong. He wants a relationship that helps him discover who he is… and who he'll become. Your child realizes this sense of significance through relationships that will never end …first with you, here on earth, and with God for all of eternity.

So… are you creating space for healthy relationships? Make your home a safe harbor from the storms of life.

hope

Scripture reminds me to not grow weary in doing good, for in due time we will reap if we surely sow. And scripture also reminds us and God has promised to complete that which he has started.   If I really didn't believe that God was who He says that He is, and that He's at work in the lives of our kids just as much as we are as parents, grandparents, brothers, sisters, or aunt or uncles, I would have given up years ago. But because I know of His involvement and the hope that He "brings to the table", I can continue to pour my life into the life of kids. Expecting nothing in return, I pour my life into kids knowing the He will cause all things to work together for good, in His timing!

There is no comment greater than this one spoken into the life of a child; "There is nothing you can do to make me love you more, and there is nothing you can do to make me love you less."

Find a child who believes his parents live this out in their life, and I'm convinced it will change the heart of any child.

hope

Continually bringing up the past to our, reminding them what they've done in the past, and never letting them forget their mistakes, eliminates any chance of hope for future change, and only gets in the way of deepening relationships.

faith...in what you know to be true.

Scripture describes God as our Heavenly Father. And I find great comfort in that for many reasons.

Teens are wired to be selfish, untrustworthy and are prone to make mistakes. But the most God-like response to that side of your child's character is to continue to love them unconditionally… just as God loves us unconditionally.

Let me be clear … loving a teen doesn't mean letting them run wild! Appropriate consequences are needed. But no mistake or blunder or selfish act should lessen your love for a son or daughter.

Hey, it comforts me to know the Heavenly Father models parenting in perfection. His grace, His mercy, His love … is a model for moms and dads … and supplies us with strength to meet the challenge.

faith

As parents, you and I want to give our kids everything, don't we?

We want to lavish our children with good things. But I'm finding a generation of teens who expect over-the-top generosity. They have a sense of entitlement that blinds them to the fact that behind every gift is a gesture of sacrifice and generosity.

And this has spiritual implications, too. In a world where teens feel like they deserve everything, the message of grace… of God's free gift… is lost.

Mom, dad, I challenge you to rethink your approach. We need to stop giving in… and help our children to understand healthy adult responses —ones that don't require demands and entitlement issues. When you do… you'll instill a deep sense of gratitude in your child.

Ever wonder if God's truly working in your kids? Or … sometimes … does it feel like He's overlooked you?

Let me offer you a fresh perspective. Maybe God is answering your prayers right now. Yeah, it doesn't feel like it, but the teen that's spiraling out of control in your home… could be the tool God uses to grow your faith!

Perhaps the conflict you're facing right now is the intentional lesson God designed specifically for you and your kids!

So, stop and think about the months in front of you. Determine right now to watch for the answers to your prayers coming your way. Don't lose heart! I promise… God's working. God's answering prayers… right in the midst of your struggle.

faith

Every day around the world… thousands of teens run away from home. No two cases are the same… but all parents who've been abandoned feel a deep sense of pain and failure.

If you've ever had a child run away from home, you know the heartache that consumes you. There's nothing like the loneliness of a quiet household… and the unanswered phone calls.

Though I can't bring your child home… I can encourage you with this: the principles you've instilled in your teen have not been wasted. The seeds you've sown in his life will come to fruition… just as the Bible promised.

Waiting for that return on investment… and the homecoming of your prodigal… will never be easy. It's your choice to wait patiently for the runaway… and cling to hope.

stepping stones II

Life has a way of dishing out trouble, doesn't it? And if you're dealing with a struggling teen in your home, I guarantee …your plate is full.

In Romans 8, we read… *And we know that all things work together for good to those who love God, to those who are called according to His purpose.* Sounds like a conflicting statement. Life dishes out trouble… and all things work together for good. Hmmm. How do we connect those dots?

Let me suggest to you that the pain of dealing with a teen spinning out of control… can lead to a new understanding of God's sovereignty. In fact, I'm guessing that last night's argument with your teen… or the tensions between the siblings… is exactly the thing that keeps you on your knees in prayer.

So, yeah …life dishes out trouble. But all things work together for those who love God. No matter what's happening in your home… God promises that He's working behind the scenes.

faith

There's no perfect formula for bringing a teenager to maturity. But… there are three ingredients that'll give you a good head start!

First. Unconditional Love lets them know there's nothing they can do to make you love them more, and nothing they can do to make you love them less.

Second. Grace gives them room to fail …and then encouragement to learn from their mistakes.

And third. Truth is the correcting influence that balances their actions with what's right and wrong. Living out the truth also means that consequences come when they step over the line!

Love, grace and truth. Take those three… flood your home and relationships with them. It's the foundation for raising healthy, godly and mature young adults.

I make this statement to teens all the time. "I owe you nothing, yet want to give you everything" It changes our relationship, their expectation, and moves me to spend more time thinking about what I have to offer, rather than what I want to take away.

faith

In a world where many daughters are more concerned about loosing their cell phone than loosing their virginity, it's important that parents engage with their daughters in such a way that brings hope into their life, and lets them know of the preciousness of their life.

James chapter 1 commands us to be "quick to listen, slow to speak, and slow to become angry." It's a tall order, isn't it? Especially with teens in the house!

I love that verse because it communicates something I see everyday. When parents jump to conclusions or begin lecturing before they've listened… it does more harm than good.

So, mom … dad …when your teen acts up, ask questions first. Be "quick to listen." Her actions may signal an issue or incident you haven't heard about yet. Maybe it's her way of communicating a loss or painful circumstance that needs attention. She's using her actions to alert you… rather than her words.

So, as James tells us, let's be quick to listen, slow to speak, and slow to become angry!

faith

Of all the billions of people on this planet, God chose you to parent your child.

Whether you have birth-children, adopted children, grandchildren or a niece or nephew… God has converged your life with theirs for a reason. That means you have unique insights, wisdom, talents, skills, and values to give your child.

In a day when kids have access to all kinds of entertainment… it's easy for parents to feel they can't compete. But kids really do want more than video games, Facebook and movies. Teens are hardwired to belong. In fact, they crave belonging! And even when they don't always show it, they crave belonging to you.

Remember… God chose you to parent your child. Make sure your teen fully understands the extent of their sacred position in your heart.

Like you, I know many families who've experienced divorce and remarriage. I know kids who've been adopted. And I know kids who are still healing from a splintered relationship with mom or dad.

If you have a blended family or perhaps one of your kids is adopted, it's important to remember that people don't heal overnight. A relational upheaval will create scars on a child's heart that can't be ignored.

It doesn't mean that blended families or adoption aren't a gift from God! They just take special care. Regardless of how good things are, your child may experience grief because of a lost relationship. And that's okay.

Remember that God is grafting together a new and beautiful family right now… that can become an infinite source of healing and joy. But healing takes time!

faith

The New Testament records the story Jesus told about a young man who left home, took his inheritance and squandered it on anything he wanted. We call him "the prodigal."

Maybe you have a prodigal in your home. A son that's wasteful, rude and greedy. Or a little drama queen who can throw the entire family into a tailspin with her outbursts of selfishness. These are prodigals who've never left the house! Why? Well, they're too comfortable!

If I'm describing your home… you may want to make a few changes. Come up with a plan to move your prodigal into adulthood. Help him or her grow up through boundaries, consequences and communication.

In Jesus' story, the prodigal grows up and comes home! That's my prayer for your teen, as well.

When parents struggle over the behavior of their teen… I encourage them to step back and take a look at the bigger picture.

No matter what's going on in your home today… it's not the whole story. The whole story is what God is up to… His "bigger picture"… which involves plans, people and purposes beyond your imagination.

I know it's hard to do… when you hurt for your child. Your struggle isn't any less important. But use this difficult season to deepen your relationship with your child… instead of simply trying to "fix" their behavior.

Place it all in God's hands. He's the one who promises to cause all things to work together for the good of those who love Him. And that's a pretty good "bigger picture"!

faith

I have three grandkids. I smile when thinking "Grandkids are a reward for not killing your own kids." My heart skips a beat every time I get to see them.

More and more I meet grandparents who've become guardians over their grandchildren. For various reasons, parents aren't able to care for the kids … and grandma and grandpa step in.

I want to encourage you … whether you're the legal caretaker for grandkids, or you just get to hang out every once in awhile … your influence is powerful! You have the opportunity to make your grandkids feel valued and to grow in confidence.

Don't miss out on these incredible occasions. If your grandkids are like mine … they love being together just as much as you do!

trust
...what you've taught & His presence in the life of your child.

stepping stones II

If anger were an art form, I think teens would be the Michelangelo's of the world!

You know what I'm talking about. The verbal tirades of a 17- year- old… the empty cussing of your child's friends… even the icy silence of a troubled teen. I might be describing some of the colorful behavior in your own home!

I've learned that many kids are upset because they're encountering things in life they weren't prepared for. The disappointment and confusion blindside them… and their response is pure anger.

Next time anger flares up in your home, be sure to keep your cool. Then …take a look behind their outrage …and try to find out what's really going on.

trust

Ever met one of those people who has a death-grip handshake? If you're not careful, they could crack the bones in your hand just by saying hello!

Sometimes moms and dads can have that vice-grip, as well. But not in a handshake… it's in the way they control their kids.

After watching a few of these parents stifle their children, I have to say that one of the hardest— but most rewarding— steps is to loosen your grip. Let your kids make decisions on their own… even if it isn't necessarily what you would've chosen for them. Let go of certain money decisions, the cleanliness of their room, or transportation issues.

You'll be surprised how your child grows when you just simply loosen your grip!

stepping stones II

Do you have a good memory? Do you have a good memory when it comes to your own shortcomings?

When you discipline your child, it's important to remember your own teenage years. Think back on the time when you dented Dad's car… or stayed out too late with friends. You grew and learned through those experiences, didn't you?

Well, now's the time to remember the life- lessons and have grace with your own children. Keep in mind that they're in process, too. Even though they may break curfew or dent the car… they're being shaped for a life of ups and downs— just like you. And chances are… they'll remember these moments for their own kids, as well!

So… a good memory is important!

trust

There's a trend called, "performance-based parenting." It's actually fairly common in homes across the country. But basing relationships on performance isn't healthy!

Performance- based parenting means that your child believes your love is conditional. If they do something wrong… you won't love them anymore. If they do something right …they you're your favor.

Now, as a mom or dad, you know that isn't true. However… we can easily communicate that way if we're not careful. If we over-emphasize academic or educational pursuits… participation in sports or religious activities… it looks like we're demanding perfection.

Is that you? Are you focused solely on performance… and don't tolerate mistakes? If so, you might want to change up your approach …and make sure you teen knows of your unconditional love.

When was the last time you asked your teenager a question … then waited for the answer? I've found that one of the most important tools in a parent's toolbox doesn't cost a thing. It's the effort to ask a question and then taking the time to listen for the answer. When I coach parents in connecting with their teen, I give them three things to think about:

> First, ask relevant questions… don't fake it.
> Second, let 'em think about the answer… don't supply it.
> And third, value their response… don't correct it.

When you do… you're communicating that you respect your teen. So, let me ask you again. When was the last time you asked your teen a really thoughtful question?

trust

There's a battle raging in homes today. It's a battle for control.

Teens want control of their lives. But I've met many parents who are afraid to let them have it. Moms will tell me their son is too immature to handle his own life. Or, dads want to teach the kid a lesson … that the world doesn't revolve around him!

Well, this battle for control is natural. But mom, dad, you can't hang on forever. The more you clamp down on your teen, the more she's tempted to control her life in other ways… like violating rules behind your back.

So be proactive! Find little ways to release your grip… to let the rope out a little. You're not losing the battle. You're training your kids to be healthy and independent!

When it comes to giving kids the freedom to make their own choices… are you afraid your children will make mistakes?

Let me ease your mind. Your kids will mess up. There's no doubt about it.

But here's the good thing. It'll give you plenty to talk about. Use their mistakes as an opportunity to help them make better decisions in the future. Let the foolish decision be useful! When your son or daughter blows it, this is your chance to value them and love them even through the pain of their mistakes. Don't shame your kids or rescue them from consequences.

Do you think your kids aren't ready to make their own choices? Of course they're not! But your teen's mistakes can be excellent teachers!

trust

One of the toughest challenges for any parent is knowing when to protect our kids…
and when to expose them to the harsh realities of the world.

There's not one of us who doesn't want to protect our children from harmful influences.
In fact, if you could drop a protective bubble over your teens, protecting them forever,
you'd do it in a heartbeat!

But the truth is, one day the bubble pops … and you're forced to relinquish control. At some point, your child needs to step out into the cruel world and start making personal choices.

So… your goal as a parent should be to move from protection to preparation. It's something that takes wisdom, a good sense of timing… and guts.

Hey …you've got what it takes. So be bold. Stop protecting …and begin preparing!

stepping stones II

Kids have a remarkable capacity to get themselves in a mess, don't they?

I've seen it a million times. A teen wants to make his own decisions, control his circumstances… and in the process, he makes a few mistakes. To a parent, it looks like he's tangled himself in a knot.

But mom and dad… before you jump in and clean up the mess… let me urge you to hold back. Part of the growing up process your son is going through right now has to do with the mess. In fact, perhaps your job right now, instead of rescuing your teen, is to hold him accountable to untangle his entanglements.

It's a lesson you once learned. And it's a lesson your teen needs to learn today, as well!

trust

Do you have a teen living at home? Then you know what it's like to watch mistakes happen.

It's inevitable. Kids make dumb choices. They'll say silly things and make a fool of themselves in front of a crowd. But you have a powerful opportunity at that crossroad. You can step in and crush them… or step in and build them up. In fact… what you say at that moment of failure describes a lot about you… and a lot about what your teen will grow up to be.

Mom. Dad. A well- timed word of encouragement in the midst of failure is worth more than an hour of praise after success.

Don't over react when your teen blows it. Be the one who holds them up when they fall.

Let me ask you a question. Are you content with whatever your teen wants to do with his or her life?

Teens often feel that they can't live up to their parents' expectations. In their mind, it's just impossible… even if your hopes are totally reasonable.

So let me ask the question again. Will you be authentically content with whatever they tell you they want to do in life? After all your hard work to get them where you think they need to be, will you be happy if they decide to pursue something other than your personal preference?

It's wise to begin talking about expectations …both from your perspective, and from your teen's point of view. Develop a heart for your teen's desires… even if it's not what you'd prefer. It's the key to keeping your relationship with your child authentic, growing and healthy.

trust

Everyone has those moments when they don't handle things well, and even the best parent loses it once in awhile. But if losing your cool has become the new normal… maybe it's time to hit the pause button… and get some help.

Ephesians 6:4 says, "Fathers, don't provoke your children to wrath." When a parent provokes their teen to the point of exasperation… it's like pouring gasoline on a smoldering fire. Furthermore, a parent's verbal barbs inflict wounds that are deep. In fact, your angry outbursts may leave scars on your teen for years to come.

So here's a challenge to you today. The next time some conflict occurs and you can feel your blood begin to boil …take a moment to gather yourself. And take this time- tested advice. It comes straight from the wisdom of Scripture: Don't provoke your children to wrath.

Matthew 6:27 says, "Can any of you add a single hour to the span of your life by worrying?"

Well, let's be honest. No matter how hard we try …it's really hard not to worry about your kids. Especially when they're acting out in unacceptable ways. It's scary to watch your child choose the wrong things, and struggle as a result.

But part of the reason God may allow your child to struggle through some things is to teach you to believe that He is in control. And that you can trust Him.

Here's another verse for you. Jeremiah 17 says … "Blessed is the man who trusts in the Lord… for he will be like a tree planted by the water… and will not fear when the heat comes. Its leaves will be green and it will not be anxious in a year of drought."

Do you find yourself weary from worry? Relax. God can be trusted.

trust

Moms and Dads, trust what you've taught your kids. Trust that the seeds of good that you've sowed into their life will one day come to fruition. Trust that all your efforts will not be returned void. Be assured that all your efforts will bring a harvest. And don't grow weary in doing good, for in due time, you will see the fruit of your efforts. God promises good things to happen in the life of your kids, and in your life.

stepping stones II

You can be certain that one day your kids will realize the uncertainty of life!

When I think about what kids view and hear today, it's no surprise that many kids entering adolescence are filled with questions. They're undecided about which path to take. They don't feel ready to face the world. And they're on the fence whether or not they buy in to the stuff their parents taught them.

The uncertainty can be overwhelming.

Moms and dads need to be aware of this anxiety simmering beneath the surface. You have an opportunity right now to step in and calm a few fears. In fact… you can be one of the certain, predictable, and constant forces in your teen's life!

trust

Remember as a kid, your mom or dad would say, "I told you so!" If you're like me, it probably didn't inspire warm fuzzies in your relationship, did it?

When you made mistakes, you didn't want to hear your mom or dad rub it in. And your kids don't wanna feel shame from you when they make mistakes either. When they've messed up, beware of using comments like …

>"You should have listened."
>"I hope you learned your lesson."
>Or… "I told you so."

You don't have to shame your kids… they already know they made a mistake. Instead, stay quiet. Let the consequences teach the lesson and continue to love your child through the entire situation.

Hey, maybe you'll be the one to break the generational saying … "I told you so!"

commitment ...to do what is right.

I meet a lot of parents who are concerned about the world's influence on their kids. And they want to raise kids that'll one day be healthy members of society. That's exactly what I want, too!

But I find that many well-meaning moms and dads think they're preparing their child for life in the world… by simply protecting them. In fact… they're over- protecting.

When that happens, kids end up either lost in a world they've never experienced before… or fighting their parents for independence. You don't want either one for your child.

commitment

I meet a lot of parents who are concerned about the world's influence on their kids. And they want to raise kids that'll one day be healthy members of society. That's exactly what I want, too!

These desires for protection and preparation are good. They're God- given tendencies for parents. But I find that many well-meaning moms and dads think they're preparing their child for life in the world… by simply protecting them. In fact… they're over- protecting.

When that happens, kids end up either lost in a world they've never experienced before… or fighting their parents for independence. You don't want either one for your child.

So the question is this: Are you preparing your teen to survive, and thrive, in the world they're about to enter?

stepping stones II

We live in a time of deep privilege. We enjoy luxuries that previous generations never did. This blessing, however, comes with responsibilities for moms and dads!

Many parents want to express their love by giving abundantly to their children. And that isn't a bad thing. But when moms and dads get into the mode of giving… giving and giving… teens begin to simply take and take! The luxuries that we know are a privilege, become what our kids demand.

I'm all for sharing. And providing for your family. But when a child acts like it's your duty to share your wealth, you need to take a step back and evaluate! After all, parenting shouldn't be about giving kids stuff to make them happy. Instead, give them a future in which they are happy.

commitment

Are you paying attention to your teen?

I find that many parents want to care for their teen better… but miss one important point of application. They don't look below the behavior and personality traits on the surface.

By the time you've had fifteen or sixteen years with a child, it's easy to assume you know him well. But now's not the time to slack off in your relationship! Dig deeper in your conversations… get to know your daughter as if you'd just met. She's growing and changing more than you can imagine… and you may find a depth and beauty below the surface that you've never seen before.

There's never been a better time to pay attention to your teen… than right now!

When it comes to moral purity …the world has changed a little since we were kids! No longer is it normal to save yourself for marriage. And the temptation to compromise looms large with our kids!

I've met with a lot of moms and dads who've learned their son or daughter is sleeping with someone. It's a scary discovery. But tolerance in today's culture has opened the door… granting teens permission to be sexually active as never before.

Teens, even though they hear a message of abstinence from mom and dad, can be overpowered by the cultural influence and driven by their own curiosity.

Mom, Dad, stay strong in your resolve. Let your voice be heard and your convictions clear. Then… make sure your kids understand you have their best interest in mind.

commitment

What if your teen made a list of his or her biggest fears …what would be at the top?

In almost 40 years of working with teens, I've learned that kids fear rejection more than anything else. And your job as a mom or dad is to show your love and acceptance… even when a son or daughter is giving nothing in return.

If you've withheld love as a disciplinary measure in the past… now's the time to stop. Withholding love and respect only increases the pain, confusion and anger your child may already feel.

Next time you're tempted to walk away, remember your teen is craving your love. Put your arm around 'em … and make sure they know …you love 'em no matter what!

stepping stones II

What does manliness look like any more? Just watch a few TV shows and you'll be as confused as the average teenager.

A few clicks of the remote and you'll find baffling trends in the male role models on television. The characters are either buffoons— portrayed as dim-witted weaklings… or they're violent and abusive. These ugly stereotypes in entertainment have actually crept into the minds of our kids… teaching them that manliness is archaic.

Moms, Dads, let's recognize the confusion this stirs up in the next generation of kids… and let's take intentional effort to model something better. Dads … live out your inner strength, courage and integrity and be all the man God created you to be.   When they're old enough to understand, your sons and daughters will thank you!

commitment

Have you ever experienced that knee-jerk reaction… when your child has done something goofy …unacceptable …and your first reaction is to pull away? Sure you have. I have, too.

We're human. And when someone hurts us… especially someone we love… it's natural to clam up. But avoiding the issues can have a disastrous impact. In fact, we become the consequence for their actions… when we pull away. That's entirely unproductive.

Mom. Dad. Though it's hard, decide right now that you'll continue to move toward your child whenever they disappoint you. Reinforce that there's nothing they can do to make you love them less… and there's nothing they can do to make you love them more.

Don't pull away. Draw them in.

One of the most powerful influences on young people today is their need to belong… to fit in and to be accepted by their peers.

Research shows that the need to belong is growing… but a sense of true belonging can't be bought. And if teens don't find a sense of belonging in their own family… they'll start looking in all the wrong places!

I've worked with thousands of kids over the years and most of them are acting out of some kind of loss… or a need to belong that was unfulfilled.

Make sure your entire family knows they have a place. Give and demonstrate unconditional love and encouragement… making sure your teen doesn't go elsewhere to find acceptance!

commitment

Think about the last time you opened your son or daughter's report card. Do you remember how you responded to their academic performance?

Whether you saw straight A's… C's, D's or F's… you had a choice in that moment about how to value your teen. See, grades are important. But we can't forget that marks don't determine a child's value. And while it's important to do well… it shouldn't overshadow our relationship.

My challenge to you is to look at the next report card… take a deep breath… then encourage your child. Help 'em work hard at school… but be sure they know that you'll love them no matter what … whether A's or F's… or anything in between.

stepping stones II

I grew up in a "three-channel" world. I'm not talking about television channels... I'm talking about communicating. Remember when there were three ways to communicate? Face-to-face conversation, a written letter or a phone call. That's it! Things have changed a bit, haven't they? Now we have countless forms of engagement ... and they're updating all the time. Most of us use the three-channel approach, but teens don't. Some of the new technology leads to a lack of deep connection. I wonder. Does your teen stick to short one-liners through text or Twitter? Have you noticed that they're great at broadcasting their thoughts, but out of practice when it comes to listening?

Maybe it's time to have a little more face-to-face time with your teen!

commitment

Parents often worry about connecting with their struggling teen. But the more I hear their stories… the more I worry about their marriage!

When your child is in pain …it's tough on mom and dad. In fact, it's exhausting …emotionally, mentally and physically. But in the midst of all those struggles, I hope you'll protect a very precious relationship. Your marriage.

When disagreements over discipline begins to infringe on your marriage relationship, take action. Immediately. Take time to get on the same page with your spouse. Remember …you are not enemies! You're working toward a common goal… and that's to move your family in a healthy direction.

So step back and take some time for your marriage. You might be surprised how it helps your struggling teen!

stepping stones II

I know something about you. You're pretty good at listening… when something is important to you.

I find that moms and dads have forgotten that fact. They don't listen any more… partly because they've gotten so good at talking. And… a few years ago when the kids were little… talking worked!

But now… when teens want to spread their wings and figure things out on their own… the time for lecturing has come to a close. Now's the time to rest your voice and use your ears. It's the perfect opportunity for you to show your teen how important you think he is.

When your teen shares his heart, don't ruin the moment by interrupting. If you do …he may quit sharing altogether!

So stop talking. And start listening!

c o m m i t m e n t

Have you set high standards for your teen? Do you want them to grow up to be smart, mature and responsible adults? Of course you do.

We all want the best for our kids. And a healthy amount of prodding and preparing are good. It's what we're called to do. But when moms and dads become more concerned with meeting the standards and lookin' good to the neighbors… bad things happen.

So don't give up on helping your teen become the best adult he can be. But watch what you're really after. If it's just the standard and making yourself look successful… better double check your motives!

Get back to loving the kid in your household …without concerning yourself with your reputation. Your teen will love you for it.

stepping stones II

There's nothing more destructive to your relationship with your child than constant lecturing.

Whenever conflict occurs, if your knee-jerk reaction is to lecture, you're communicating that you don't think your teen can think for himself. And if you condemn him for his mistakes, you're actually reinforcing that you don't really respect him.

That's not your intent …but it's what your child is hearing.

So what can be done? Well, stop lecturing and start listening. In fact, start today! Right now, even. Try it for a day. Don't flip out, argue or lecture. Button up your lips. Just let it go. It'll take a lot of discipline on your part, but you may discover it's just what your teen needs.

Then watch what happens. Before long …your teen will return the favor and start listening to you!

commitment

It's one of the most insidious traps parents fall into.

I'm talkin' about comparison. Yep, it's easy to look at some one else's family and use them as a measuring stick. They eat dinner together every night. Looks like a Norman Rockwell painting. Your family's lucky if they grab stale pizza before running out the door.

The other kids never speak an unkind word… they're always obeying mom and dad. But your kids, of course, seem to be testing the boundaries all day long!

Let me calm your nerves a little here. That other family? They're not as good as they look. And… it's not worth getting caught up in comparison! Mom and dad… get back to watching your own kids. They're exactly what God wants for you today!

stepping stones II

When I was a kid, the music I liked drove my parents crazy. They couldn't understand why I liked what they called "noise."

You might not like the music your teen listens to, either. But I meet a lot of parents who make a big deal out of a small issue. They major on the minors. Even though you may not like a particular type of music… step back and take stock. Is the choice of music… or whatever else you're dealing with today… the thing that should fracture your relationship?

It's amazing how your teen's taste will change over time. Before long, they might even like much of the same music you and I do. So… make sure you're focusing on the majors. Not the minors!

patience

...in doing what you know is right.

stepping stones II

I don't spend too much time in the kitchen… I prefer to barbeque on the back porch. But I do know that recipes make baking a whole lot easier. The problem comes when we apply the step-by-step process to raising kids!

Adding ingredients in the right order and giving it time in the oven may work in the kitchen… but you're in trouble if you think that's the way parenting works!

Raising mature and independent adults takes intentionality. Focus on building a relationship, listening to your teen, and sticking to your boundaries. This will be an ongoing process… long after your kids leave the home.

Remember, parenting doesn't take a simple recipe… it takes a mindset. And it takes time.

patience

When they say, "the apple doesn't fall far from the tree" …they aren't necessarily referring to personality types.

Just because a child shares your last name and reflects your facial features… doesn't mean they have a similar personality type. You may be calm, cool and collected… while your son is boisterous and the life of the party. You might be into sports… while your daughter would rather play clarinet in the band.

Neither personality is bad! It just takes extra effort on your part to accept your child as he is… to resist forcing him into your own likes and dislikes.

When it comes to the apple falling far from the tree… celebrate the differences in your kids!

Have you ever given in to a teen's tantrum… just to keep the peace in your house? It may work for a while… but in the long term, it's never a good idea!

I've heard parents say a very dangerous statement: As long as my kid gets what he wants, everything is just fine. But the minute they're refused something, all chaos breaks loose.

When I hear that… it tells me that these parents are keeling to their teen's outbursts. They're making a ditch effort to keep peace in the home… but it comes at a high price. Because placating tantrums only leads to more tantrums… and manipulative behavior that only grows more insidious through the years.

So, if you've been keeping peace at all costs in your home… I challenge you to count the long- term ramifications. And don't let tantrums slide!

patience

You've made a few mistakes in your life, haven't you?

No one gets through life without a few blunders. But I still run into many parents who don't want their kids to mess up at all. They keep them from participating in any sports or activity… just so they won't fall on their face. Or… mom and dad make every decision for their teen… so he doesn't have a chance to choose poorly.

That, my friends… is a recipe for disaster!

It's important for moms and dads to remember that just as we made poor decisions growing up, our kids will do the same. And when they do… give a big hug and remind your son or daughter how much you love them anyway!

Learning from our mistakes is the only path to becoming an independent adult.

stepping stones II

Teen behavior doesn't always make sense. And if you have a teenager in your home… you know exactly what I mean.

All teen behavior is goal- oriented. They behave certain ways because they're trying to reach their goal… and meet a need. That doesn't mean we can always understand what they're doing or why they're doing it… but it does give us a foundation from which to start.

Begin by thinking through the needs. What is it your child longs for? Maybe he just wants someone to notice him. Perhaps she wants to cover up private pain or find a measure of peace. Take time to examine your teen's hidden motivations.

Don't be distracted by the way they behave … even if it doesn't make sense. Instead, look for their heart-felt longings!

patience

Take a moment to think about what's preoccupying your thoughts today. Worried about something? Muscles a little tense? How ya doing on stress management?

Everyone has stress at some level. It's natural. And it comes from a million different sources. But for parents of teens, the hassle meter peaks a little higher than normal! Constant emotional tension, agitation and conflict can kick it up a few notches.

So mom and dad, make a conscious effort to manage the pressure. Figure out how to combat that nagging tension you feel between your shoulders. Exercise. Get away. Laugh a little. Take a Sabbath.

Keeping yourself healthy will actually defuse family stress. And who knows? Maybe you'll all begin laughing again!

stepping stones II

No two teens are alike. They're designed by God to be unique and dynamic. Even two teens, under one roof, sharing the same mom and dad… will be radically different from each other!

There are external differences, of course… blue eyes versus brown. But I'm talking about personalities. What works for one teen won't work for all the kids at home. When one feels comfortable in a new situation, another might shy away from it. One kid may explode in anger… the other might comply silently.

It's important to know the differences in your kids… and adapt for each one. You might want to employ different techniques. Ask questions… so you know how to tweak your parenting style to fit.

It'll take a extra effort … but it'll be worth it all! Celebrate that no two teens are alike!

patience

I meet a lot of parents who wonder why their teen is so irresponsible. Hey, teens will always act immature …because they're still growin' up. But sometimes… mom and dad are getting' in the way.

Are you an overly responsible parent? Raising an irresponsible teen? Mom …dad… when you do everything for your kid… it does nothing more than postpone his or her potential to grow up. In fact, when you step in and protect them from the natural consequences to their behavior… you're actually stifling creativity and limiting motivation!

So take a step back. Let go of all the stuff you're doing on their behalf. Quit trying to rescue your teen from the hard knocks of life. Who knows? If you step out …they just might step up!

stepping stones II

I once heard my friend Jim Burns say … "Listening is the language of love." I couldn't agree more.

If you have a teen who's struggling, it's likely you've given him some advice… or even explained the right direction to go. But if he's like the teens I've met …he isn't really paying attention to you. Am I describing your son or daughter?

Mom. Dad. I know you have good intentions. And you're not trying to lecture. But you need to figure out how to communicate your love in a different way. Love your teen by listening!

It won't be easy. And you may hear some things you don't like. But by sitting down and opening your ears… you'll say more to your son or daughter than you ever dreamed!

patience

It's a topic many of us would rather dodge. It can make both parents and children alike squirm.

I'm talking about our sexually- charged culture. The temptations for inappropriate sexual expression and experimentation abound. And though it's easier to assume that your kids are making right choices… there's no substitute for a healthy one- on- one conversation.

Mom. Dad. Empower your kids to make wise choices by opening up the dialogue at home. No subject should be off limits.

How soon? At what age to you broach the subject? That's a question you have to answer. But I'll tell you this. It's probably sooner than you think!

stepping stones II

What do you want your kids to be like in ten or fifteen years? What qualities are you hoping they'll acquire? With that in mind… how should you train your child today… to reach that long- range goal?

As a mom or dad of a teenager, it's easy to get caught up in the day-to-day pressures of managing a family. Your target should be to raise a responsible adult… not necessarily a compliant teenager.

So when you're in the heat of the battle …keep your eyes on the horizon. A weak and docile teenager might simplify your life. But becoming a responsible adult is far better. And some days … it may get messy.

Hang in there. Your hard work will deliver rich rewards!

patience

Proverbs 22:6 says, "Train up a child in the way he should go and when he is old, he will not turn from it."

That's a comforting promise for parents. But I know some moms and dads who want the "he will not turn from it" part to happen immediately. My response is this: now's a really good time to work on your patience!

When your child walks away from the values and beliefs you've instilled… it's painful. I know. But take courage. Journeys don't happen overnight, and God's leading your child on a path that may take the long way around.

I hope you'll continue to hold on to that promise… even when times are tough. "Train up a child in the way he should go and when he is old, he will not turn from it."

Studies show that kids who grow up in the church are actually abandoning their faith in record numbers… especially when they hit the late teen years. Why is that?

As you know, our world is changing. It's no longer socially expected to attend church. Quite the opposite, in fact. Your teen hears anti- church messages all day long.

Mom, dad … this will be an uphill battle. Expect difficulty when you value something that the world doesn't value. Avoid the temptation to mock or berate your teen … as they strive to establish their own spiritual convictions.

And by all means, don't give up! Keep encouraging your kids to pursue the truth, to connect with other Christians… and remember … there's nothing more winsome than a mom or dad who truly loves God with all their heart!

patience

The mark of a good parent is not necessarily a good kid who never gets into trouble, makes a bad decision, or fails a class.

The mark of good parenting is not only determined by the way a child acts at home during their teen years… but also how a child engages and responds during their adult years. You see, this is a marathon… not a fifty- yard dash!

Your teen may make some embarrassing mistakes, but when you move toward them in love, even when it's hard … you'll sow the seeds for a healthy relationship that endures for years.

Hey, wouldn't you want a well-balanced adult child who messed up in his teens… rather than a perfect kid who fell apart in his thirties?

Remember, this is a marathon, not a sprint.

Nobody's perfect. Nobody makes it through life without hurting others… and getting hurt in the process. Relationships are messy.

If you have a teen in your family, you know what it feels like to be hurt, disrespected or ignored. But you have a choice in the middle of all this. You can love your kids, even when you feel like they don't deserve it.

Like I said. Relationships are messy. And I've learned over the years that if I walk away from someone every time they offend me… I allow their actions to determine the future of our relationship. That's not what any parent wants.

This time around… choose to show love… even when the kids don't deserve it.

patience

When traveling to a foreign country, you may employ a translator… someone to help you understand what's going on around you. Well, for some of us, it seems like our kids are speaking a foreign language right at home! Need help understanding what's going on?

I've met a lot of parents who give well- meaning advice to their children… but it's interpreted much differently than it was intended. The kid barks some kind of defensive comment… and parents are left wondering, What did I say wrong?

At this point it's helpful to put yourself in your teen's shoes… to "translate" your comments, if you will. You might be surprised that your well- intentioned comments actually came across as judgmental.

Next time, pause and translate your comments before you speak!

I once asked the kids what they wished their parents knew. One student said, "No matter how deep a hole I got into, I didn't want my parents to leave me."

Another student said, "I wish they knew that their definition of abnormal was my definition of normal." And one more. A teenage boy said to me "Just because I don't talk doesn't mean I don't want to. It's just that I don't know what to say."

Maybe it's time you ask your own teen that question: What do you wish your parents knew?

loving When It's Hard…and you're
ready to give up.

stepping stones II

Struggling teens often present a crisis to their parents. Mom and dad might back away from their child in those moments… because they feel like failures. Or they jump in and protect their teen from any hardship… longing to give them an easy and good life.

My challenge to moms and dads with struggling teens is this: As your kids apply the principles you've taught them, they'll always run into trouble in the world. But that doesn't mean you've done your job poorly! In fact… it's your chance to step up and love your teen at the time they need you most.

Struggle is normal. It's healthy. And you need to expect it in your teen!

loving

I meet a lot of responsible parents. They prepare for everything… from financial uncertainty to disaster readiness. But when it comes to conflict in the home, they're hopelessly unprepared!

Conflict isn't optional in homes… it will come, especially if you have teens under your roof! So, one of the best things you can do as a mom or dad is be prepared. But how?

Well, first, it's important to decide that you'll move toward your teen, no matter what the fight is about. Communicating love is more important than winning every argument.

Then, before any fight breaks out, make a plan for how you'll listen and stay focused on the topic at hand. When you get sidetracked or stop listening, the conflict inevitably goes downhill.

So… are you prepared for battle?

Every mother or father wants their child to do well in life. And teens benefit from a healthy push once in awhile. But I'd caution you against pushing for perfection!

The focus with your teen should not be about success or failure in their activities. Instead, it's about continuing to love your child through his difficulties.

Well, what does that really look like? First, make sure your child knows that he's valued, no matter what he does. Second, make a habit of starting conversations with your child that have nothing to do with their performance. Ask questions about how she feels… or what he's facing.

You'll broaden the base of your conversations… and reinforce that you love your teen …no matter what!

loving

The greatest message that you can give your child is this:

There is nothing you can do to make me love you more; and there is nothing you can do to make me love you less.

A child, whether an infant, toddler, grade schooler, tween, teen, post-teen, young adult or a new mother or father, longs to know of this type of love. And I believe that a parent, whether a new one, an aged one, or a grand parent (and even grand parents) long to have this type of love with a child.

You can send this message to someone today. You can stop what you're doing right now, and send this message that can change the heart of any person.

stepping stones II

Change isn't easy. In fact, most people hate change!

The thought of making changes at home is scary and challenging. We keep doing things the way we've always done them… and getting out of the rut takes energy and cramps our style.

Another reason people don't like change is that it's often preceded by conflict. But let me turn this on its head: conflict that leads to change can be a good thing. It might be just what your family needs!

When the rut you're in eventually leads to the wrong place relationally… it's worth the work to get out of it! I challenge you today to see conflict and change as good things… even though they're hard.

loving

When moms and dads are in the thick of it… when every day brings up a new conflict and teens seem to change personality by the week… it's hard to keep the goal in mind.

The goal is this: Mom and dad, you are preparing your child to function independently in the world! You're giving her the skills she needs to live an autonomous life. So… how do you reach for that goal today? Well…

> Don't be afraid to let disappointment and rejection into your child's life.
> They've got to face it sometime!
>
> And talk through the conflicting messages of our culture…
> don't isolate them to a protective bubble.
>
> Finally, demonstrate commitment and character in your personal life.
> You're a bigger role model than you think!

Take a positive step toward your goal every day… and begin releasing your child into the world as a healthy, balanced adult!

Most of us have the luxury of walking away from tough situations or people who tick us off. We can quit our job… or bail on a relationship. But teens under our care don't have the same freedom.

For the most part… teens are a captive audience. At least when it comes to attending school and living under our roof. When they get frustrated or angry… they're forced to live with the person who caused the disruption.

For many teens, that means they'll choose to fight. Lash out. When backed into a corner, they'll attempt to inflict pain on their offender.

So next time your teen gets hot … try to give them grace. It's quite possible they feel stuck. Don't get sidetracked by their outbursts. Help them work through the pain!

loving

When it seems like nothing's goin' right at home… when your teen is spinning out of control… ever feel like throwing up your hands and walking away?

Yeah, raising healthy kids is tough business. And I meet a lot of parents who are confused, tired and frustrated. They long for easier days.

Well, there's no one who can wave a magic wand over your household and make it all better… but there is One who can change you from the inside out. So when you feel like giving up… it's the perfect time to depend on God.

So instead of getting hassled over the trials at home … turn to the only One who can help you. See this as a grand adventure for God to do His greatest work … in you.

Teens today feel a sense of entitlement. They want more, demand more, and expect more than any other generation I've known.

My friend, Dr. Tim Kimmel, puts it this way: "The problem with kids brought up in our typical middle class home is this… they're born on third base but are under the delusion they hit a triple!"

It's this platform of unbridled entitlement that causes young people to remain immature, neglect responsibility and treat people disrespectfully. Basically… they're refusing to grow up.

Sadly, I often see moms and dads fostering these attitudes in their children. There's nothing wrong with wanting to give your child things, and put 'em on third base… but consider how withholding privileges might teach your child much more than hitting a grand slam!

loving

No one makes it through life without dealing with this human emotion. Loss.

The pain that follows loss is something none of us escape. It's overwhelming when you've lost something or someone. You know what it's like to grieve a broken relationship or spend sleepless nights fretting over the loss of a dream.

Well, those same painful feelings are stirred up in your teen, as well. When they don't get what they want… or their dreams are shattered… they experience the hollowness of disappointment, too. But unlike adults …teens rarely know how to express it.

So keep your eyes open for grief in your teen's life. Watch how they fill that void… and always be ready to give 'em a hug! All of us need those arms of affection that remind us everything's gonna be okay.

stepping stones II

Kids require correction. From their toddler years to their teenage years, they need guidance nd discipline.

For the most part, I meet parents who have discipline down pat. They know how to instruct, enforce and correct. But where they fall short… is the relationship. They tend to mistake arguments for conversation and living under the same roof for spending quality time together.

But without having a deep and lasting connection with your teen— before the need for discipline arises— you'll find your eloquent lectures entirely ineffective!

If your relationship with your son or daughter is broken or damaged… take time repair it. Your pearls of wisdom can only be received when it comes from a foundation of a healthy relationship.

loving

Do you have many battles in your home? Are there bunkers built up throughout the house?

You may find that the frequency and intensity of scuffles are increasing in your home. If so, I'd encourage you to think about the hills you're dying on. Ask yourself a few questions:

> What issues have the greatest consequences?
> What battles, if you lose, will also cause you to sacrifice a relationship?
> What battles will eventually pass?

Once you've answered these questions… adjust what you fight back about. Reevaluate what' really important to you.

Mom, dad, choose your battles carefully. Don't pounce on every little mistake. On the essential non-negotiable stuff…don't budge one inch! On the non-essentials…show a little grace and mercy.

Conflict comes in many forms. Sometimes it explodes in boiling bursts of anger. Other times it comes over the house like a sheet of ice… sending a chill across your relationships. So… what's the temp in your household today?

I'd challenge you to take a positive view of conflict . Whether it's heated debate with your teens… or awkward silence… consider this …

If you've ever prayed to be the parent God has called you to be… that's what He's doing. Right now. The process may throw you off balance… but conflict with your kids may be refining your character in ways you never imagined.

So …no matter the temperature in your household …trust God to guide you… and help you make the most of His refining work in you!

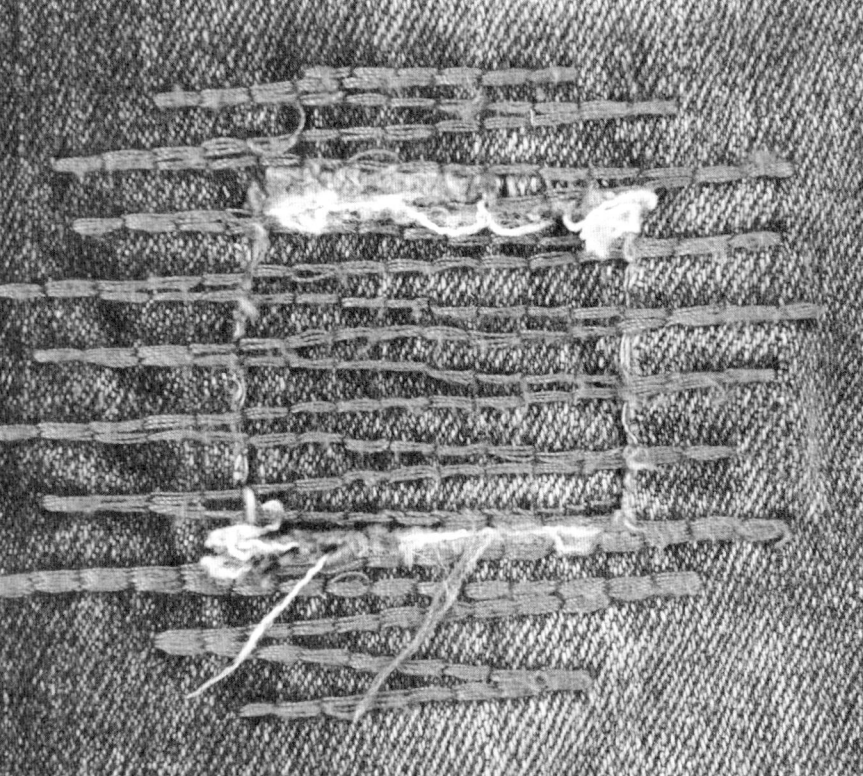

restoration of relationships you hold dear.

stepping stones II

Is there an age where it's too late to "fix" things?

Maybe you're at a place where you feel like there's no going back. What's done is done. It seems like your kids have gone off the deep end… and now they're even out of the house.

It's never too late. God is always working in you, in the situation and in your child. But you may have to set aside the idea of "fixing" anything.

Perhaps now's the time for you, as a mom or dad, to trust God… to let Him bring about the restoration you desperately want …and only He can do.

restoration

No relationship survives without forgiveness. In fact, for parents, it's needed on a daily basis!

Whether you have toddlers running around the home, or you're working through the issues of adolescence with your son or daughter… you know about forgiveness. And, most likely, you know what happens when you don't forgive. The bitterness that comes when we hold onto the pain is destructive, to say the least.

But you have a choice right now. You can choose, by God's grace, to let go of how your teen hurt you… and begin to rebuild the relationship that has suffered. It's possible! But it'll take making that choice every day.

So start right now. Choose to forgive.

stepping stones II

Forgiveness is giving up hope that you'll ever have a better past.

restoration

Through the years I've seen many good relationships go bad, turn stale, and become "distanced" because of the stubbornness of either person to extend a hand of grace to the other to help each other the divisive wall or hurt and pain. What a shame to see something that could be so good, go so bad. Maybe today's the time to make that call to that person on the other side of your wall?

stepping stones II

Men and women are very different creatures. We see things differently, we respond to crisis differently… and we often parent differently.

After several decades working with families, I've seen a huge diversity in the approach moms and dads use …when it comes to dealing with their teens. Moms tend to talk more… and want to fix everything in a single conversation. Dads tend to avoid working through conflict… and don't say enough. Sound familiar?

Well, even though we wrestle with different issues in the home… there's no substitute for the viewpoints we bring. Use your distinction as an asset. Celebrate the unique relationship you both enjoy with your kids.

The best homes are those where moms are moms and dads are dads.

restoration

Small changes in a home can make a world of difference. For instance, when a child begins to enter adolescence, begin switching your parenting mode from teaching to training, from lecture to discussion, and from giving answers to creating an atmosphere where they must find the answer. Small changes can turn the heart and attitude of your child toward you in an amazing short period of time. The great distance felt between relationships can be shortened with small and seemingly insignificant changes in the way that you engage with your kids.

How's the chemistry with the people in your house? Are you truly connecting? And how's your relationship with your teen?

After thirty-plus years of working with struggling teens and their families… I've come to realize that almost everything goes back to relationship. A discipline problem is usually a relationship problem. Conflict becomes an enemy when there's no connection between parent and child. And rules in your home that aren't backed by a strong sense of rapport will eventually yield rebellion.

Are you convinced yet? Hey, there's no better time than right now to work on connecting with your teen. No matter how you've blown it in the past, no matter how much tension is building, it's never too late to pursue relationships at home.

restoration

How does your teen see you? Does she know you love her? Does he get that you've made mistakes, too?

It's not uncommon to find a mom or dad who wants to come across to their teen like they've got it all together. They don't want to be seen making mistakes… or having to apologize.

But one of the things I think is healthy for parents and teens… is honesty. In fact, let your teenager see that you have shortcomings and setbacks. It'll cause two things to happen. First, they'll cut you some slack… because no one is perfect. Then, they'll be more realistic about themselves.

I hope that together… you and your teen can give each other grace. You'll both have your mistakes. But admitting your weaknesses only deepens your relationship!

stepping stones II

When was the last time you humbled yourself … and spoke those two giant words … I'm sorry?

I once witnessed an entire family break down and sob when the father asked each member to forgive him for the way he'd handled himself in their relationship. He extended the olive branch with intensity and emotion.

It was a humble, sincere apology, and a good step toward restoring his position with his children. Every heart in the room melted …and anger and resentment began to lift.

I challenge you to take the dad's example. Do you need to admit responsibility for building walls in your family? For contributing to miscommunication? It's time to start steering your home in the right direction, and fostering respect in those you love.

Your teen may seem like a fortress with high walls and a locked gate. Impenetrable. But seeking forgiveness may unlock the door to his or her heart. Just say those two powerful words … I'm sorry.

restoration

Let me ask you a question. How did you learn to forgive?

It's not something most of us think about. But I'd wager that you weren't taught to forgive… you just "caught" it from your parents. You learned by their actions what it meant to forgive and forget. The sad part is… if they held grudges… you most likely do, too.

Forgiveness isn't easy. In fact it's impossible without God's help. And when you're hurt by someone— especially your children— it's tempting to hold back love. The problem here is that you're teaching your kids two things: first, they're only lovable when they don't mess up… and second, that they'll treat their own kids like that.

So break the cycle. Trust God and offer forgiveness!

stepping stones II

It's a question I get asked a lot! "Should I tell my teen about the mistakes in my past?"

You and I made a lot of mistakes when we were growing up. Some were small and stupid. Others were bigger than we realized… and even changed the direction of our lives! So… should we share with our kids some of these secret mishaps? Or will that simply lead to an excuse for them to repeat the cycle?

Well, in my experience, I've found that honesty about the past… in age appropriate ways, of course… actually leads to a stronger relationship. Kids will know you're not perfect, and you can share the real regret you feel for some of your poor choices.

HeartlightMinistries
ESTABLISHED 1988

Located on 100 acres in the piney woods of East Texas, Heartlight provides a residential setting for adolescents 13 to 17 years old, who are in desperate need of an alternative residential setting. This year-round program provides a therapeutic setting for 60 young men and women. The staff is passionate about their work with struggling teens, and committed to excellence in every facet of providing an atmosphere of relationships that creates an arena for change. When a parent's attempt to solve family crisis is not working, Heartlight offers an alternative for families that brings hope to parents and teens alike.

For more information about the Heartlight residential counseling program please call the Heartlight office at 903.668.2173, or visit HeartlightMinistries.org.

"HEARTLIGHT SAVED OUR DAUGHTERS LIFE."

parenting TODAY'S TEENS
with MARK GREGSTON

Parenting Today's Teens Radio is heard on more than 1,400 stations across North America, and is dedicated to providing practical, biblical advice to parents of teens and pre-teens. Produced by Roger Kemp & Company, each broadcast consists of teachings by Mark Gregston, coupled with interviews with special guests, all addressing a particular topic relevant to today's teens. PTT Radio speaks to the issues facing parents today, and gives practical advice on dealing with the effects of the current teen culture.

To find a station carrying the daily and weekend radio programs, visit www.ParentingTodaysTeens.org. You can also find podcasts of all of our radio broadcasts on iTunes. Parenting Today's Teens can be heard nationwide on XM/Sirius Satellite on channel 131, the Family Talk channel, every Saturday at 1:00 pm (CST) or Sunday at 3:00 pm (CST).

For news, tip, links and resources, follow us on Twitter at www.twitter.com/markgregston and Facebook at www.facebook.com/parentingteens.

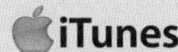 

www.ParentingTodaysTeens.org

"THESE E-MAILS SEEM TO COME JUST WHEN I NEED THEM MOST! THANKS MUCH FOR THE WONDERFUL WORDS OF ENCOURAGEMENT."

When you sign up for the e-mail Parenting Tips Newsletter, you'll receive a weekly article featuring issues facing parents of teens today. Included are new products, upcoming events, and a calendar of Mark Gregston's scheduled appearances and events. You'll also have an opportunity to read about the upcoming Parenting Today's Teens weekend radio program.

To sign up for the weekly e-mail newsletter, visit **www.ParentingTodaysTeens.org**

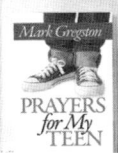
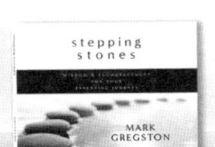

HELP FOR PARENTS OF TEENS IS HERE.

DVD & CD sets
Retreats & Conferences
Informative Booklets
Curriculum Kits
Reference Books
Radio Broadcasts

www.pttresources.com